THE USABLE FIELD

Also by Jane Mead

House of Poured-Out Waters
The Lord and the General Din of the World
A Truck Marked Flammable (chapbook)

The Usable Field

JANE MEAD

ALICE JAMES BOOKS
FARMINGTON, MAINE

10 9 8 7 6 5 4 3 2 1

Alice James Books are published by Alice James Poetry Cooperative, Inc.,
an affiliate of the University of Maine at Farmington.

Alice James Books
238 Main Street
Farmington, ME 04938

www.alicejamesbooks.org

Library of Congress Cataloging-in-Publication Data

Mead, Jane
 The usable field / Jane Mead
    p. cm.
 ISBN-13: 978-1-882295-69-2
 ISBN-10: 1-882295-69-2
 I. Title.

PS3563.E165U83 2008
811'.54--DC22
                        2008014275

Alice James Books gratefully acknowledges support from the University of
Maine at Farmington and the National Endowment for the Arts. ❧

Cover art: Watercolor landscape of the flats at Mead Ranch
by Chris Jorgensen (1860-1935).

For Giles Mead

(1928-2003)

In memoriam

ACKNOWLEDGMENTS

∾

Grateful acknowledgement is made to the editors of the following journals and anthologies, in which some of these poems first appeared, sometimes in earlier versions: *American Poetry Review, Blink, Canary River Review, The Bread Loaf Anthology of New American Poets, Chicago Review, The Dirty Napkin, Electronic Poetry Review, Excerpt, "For New Orleans" & Other Poems, Great River Review, Greensboro Review, The Indiana Review, Joyful Noise: An Anthology of American Spiritual Poetry, Ploughshares, Poetry, Poetry Daily, Pool, TriQuarterly, Underwood Broadside Series, Washington Square* and *Web Del Sol*.

In addition, I am most grateful to the John Simon Guggenheim and Patrick Lannan Foundations for invaluable and timely support in the form of a fellowship and a writing residency.

To Brian Teare, Larissa Szporluk, Cort Day, Jennifer Chandler, Dennis Sampson: thank you for being there, with your gentle friendship and your sharp minds. Special thanks to Jan Weissmiller, who has helped shape these poems and this book with great insight and tireless generosity.

Silvia and Ramon Rodriguez, Judi Ouellette: thank you for keeping the wheels turning.

CONTENTS

The Dead, Leaning (in the Grasses
and Beyond the Trenches,— Like Oaks)

I

II

III

THE DEAD, LEANING (IN THE GRASSES AND BEYOND THE TRENCHES,—LIKE OAKS)

In the high and mighty grasses
the dead lean on the living
like nobody's business,—

they think we are their mission.
Thus the rain, whereby they say
now wash your eyes and pray.

Pray for anything but forgiveness.

In the trenched terrain the shadows
in people identify with mountains—
the people have to be rodents

if they want to debate. Else,
there's just the undignified
nature of revenge, inheritance

and innuendo, being and dint—
not even a breeze to soften
the ought. For this is the tumor

of living among them—
if there is death between you
and the oak, there is no oak.

I

To Whatever Remains

This is some chant I'm working at—
tired on tarmac and disaster,
best I can do these days is hope

for some way to keep the rote days rote.
Hard to tell what's safe,
hard to tell what's wise. Fog means:

unlock the geese from the sky—at your
own risk, at your peril.
But the truth is I pass that harp

to the disappeared soul, saying soul
sing me something, speak of the
best dream—that's a beginning.

Tired on tarmac, this keeps me going—
but barely. Where's the disaster
that would be enough? What's that beauty

in the last light leaving for the day?
Anything to do with how I-880 tops the hill
and heads on down toward San Jose?

Soul, sing me something of how the good earth
heals. Sing me something soon. As if
being asked to celebrate created things.—

As if being passed the harp and asked to sing.
Do it before the crow at the dog bowl exits.
Do it before life goes taut as a new scar.

Before the fog lifts, before the geese
fly over in Air Force formation.

SOME DAYS

I hide in the river
with a reed to breathe through.
The river carries me

slowly downstream.
Luna calls it the bit
where I converse with slime.

She says it's just a part
of a larger step, she says
she can't believe I don't

know how the dance goes.

AND THEN THE SMOKE —

sole residue of written wisdom
as actualized by things.
Christ if the tulips shudder.

Here the grass is rain-flattened
and may not re-spring. What
can one person say to another?

The master is the master?
The children are playing on the shore?
To this language, the heron on the sandbar

does not answer.
Objects sought after.
Objects retrieved.

The season of rain passes.
The master is not the master.

THREE CANDLES
AND A BOWERBIRD

I do not know why
the three candles must sit
before this oval mirror,

but they must.—
I do not know much
about beauty, though

its consequences
are clearly great—even
to the animals:

to the bowerbird
who steals what is blue,
decorates, paints

his house; to the peacock
who loves the otherwise
useless tail of the peacock—

the tail *we* love.
The feathers *we* steal.
Perhaps even to the sunflowers

turning in their Fibonacci
spirals the consequences
are great, or to the mathematical

dunes with ripples
in the equation of all things
windswept. Perhaps

mostly, then, to the wind.
Perhaps mostly to the bowerbird.
I cannot say.

But I light the candles: there is
joy in it. And in the mirror
also, there is joy.

THE RIVER ITSELF

Gretel chomps the shadow
of a crow, and the crow
falls—as the crow flies,

so to speak—into
the smashed corn.
Some of this happens

in a field, some
in the quarter-pounder
that is Gretel's brain.

Also there is a bus
caught on a bend in the river.
The bus needs work.

Let me introduce myself:
I am Luna, keeper of the dachshund,
the dachshund Gretel

to be precise. One of the sorriest
shapes man ever thought up
when it comes to stomping

the muddy fields.
But talk about swimming—
Gretel swims like an angel.

Gretel is,
to be precise,
a short-leggèd angel.

I myself am Luna.
Wind.
There's a storm

named after me—just look
what it has done
to the banks of this river—.

Regard the ill-fated bus
and ask me if I give a damn.
Say *Luna, do you give a damn?*

I say crow.
I say wind.
It's a river.

I say look at the light
playing on the earth—
and take it, so to speak,

with a grain of salt.
Or take it elsewhere—
Gretel would.

WE TAKE THE CIRCUS
TO ANOTHER LEVEL —

we, who are not afraid to die,—we remember how
to love nothing. No blue jay in the pepper tree, no
crocus blooming on the compost, and most steadfastly

no rye-grass-swaying-in-breezes. No breezes.
No fetish of turtle carved from jade. The palmist
says *trees together, trees apart: the odds*

by definition can't conspire. Still, we are
the future in which the ankle breaks. We keep
records of what is harvested and what is due

and the records own us, who never think of elsewhere
as a mission. In our unhurried gloom, we are just
a grave away from the truth: the mechanism

of grief supplies no answer. *Hearts empty*
says the palmist, *hearts with blood in them.*
The act of grieving is not required.

The odds, by definition, can't conspire.

You Are Not Removed

until the light
    washes over you—

and the light has *not*
    washed over you.

You need to love the gnats
    swirling over the toxic

swamp (for the swamp is *always*
    toxic) you need to

catalogue mazes and map
    adamancies, get

chokecherries to grow
    next to sage—

unleash even
    the slightest allegiance

and *then* let the light
    wash over you.

The Part — and the Whole of It

Stocking the globe is not
my issue, taking stock
is my issue—and deciding

what to do next. I was
only a speck until the machine
got a hold on me. I'd curl up

and read my accounts. It was
another world—built on dead trees—
on the shores of mirror and veil.

Now—men and women speaking:
Same audit, same flinch.
Same tongue—no visible shore.

Home is another story:
different specks, same machine.
Prescription or sacrifice—

it's hard to say, but always
the same relentless fever—
on the tattered wing of day.

WOODS HOLE

Window to the sea. Bells
are ringing. The road
to the south is blue—

all over the dunes
rose-hips bloom. All
over town—bells. Many

are the ways, but there
is only one road
home, and it is not

for you. All over
town—and the road
to the south is blue.

GIFT HORIZON

Turn the head of the bird he says
and dies, leaving us in the rain
and his painting unfinished. Turn

the head of the bird. We haven't
got a clue (and it raining)—so, slowly,
we learn to love moss and even the sheen

of green algae inside the water trough. Not
a clue and it always (the trough)
suggesting a future of gray horses—

the trail muddy, the child bruised
long before the shadowy race begins.
Nor is the woman singing, she's crying.

He painted her as if singing because
he was broken and would have stolen
anything to heal himself.

POINT AND COUNTERPOINT
IN ALL THINGS

It is easy for the mind
to hold *magnolia* in its wings
at a time when the magnolia

is blossoming,—scattering its famous
petals, (famous white, rimmed
with famous brown) around your doorstep—.

It is easy to understand the importance
of linen or to give of yourself
until there is no self. But when the book

is opened to the page about magnolias
then where will you be? There is
a talisman called *mercy*, there is

a single blossom—called *commence*.

SISTER HARVEST
BROTHER BLUES

Because there is no earth-light,
because there is none other, we remain
wayward and hampered. No one

will be going this day with us.
The main force is the usable field
or sun on the useless bunchgrass,—

alchemy that spells and spells us
just as the weather spells us
and the good earth *field*. Rain

by morning and the earthworms
surface. Meanwhile, gathering
facts enough for continued serving:

mosquito-fish for the horse trough,
dented washtub by the spring
where the deer drink, drowned rat

bald and bloated in the barrel
by the stream. What is the science *for*
that leads us doe-eyed into the source

of our unmaking? Or, at the source
there is an answer—? Manufactured
instincts, and on the lawn now roughly

thirty-seven strong and busy starlings.

ALL WADING HAS WINGS

A picnic by the river
would be the right
thing, despite the secret

holding water, secret
holding of water—then
not, and the day

holding its hours
then not, then the moon
through which you see

the fish and rocks—
forgetting sometimes
even about the water.

By Reason of Light—

There have been many—
Who called in the ships.—
Ships in off the dark water.

Instinct one minute—
Satire the next.—
There have been many.

From one vision to the next—
It is a long distance.
You have to carry a moth through rain.

You have to sleep under an upturned boat.
You have to actually *be* there.
As in *willing to die for same.*

And you have to be willing to live.
As in *I will trade you tomorrows*—.
As in no known shore, no meaning.

If the Field Is Real

Early in this summer
of the old trees blowing down
I plant flowers—send

the dead away, one by one,
and plant flowers. We are,
now, township by township—

rough at the edges, trees
snapped, brush burning.
I plant flowers—send

the dead away, one by one.
Half my oak down, half
trying to live, mulberry

rough at the edges, trees
snapped, brush burning—
a statue of splinters.

I mow the field—
half my oak down, half
trying to live, mulberry

where the chipmunk hid. I burn
what is left of my trees—
a statue of splinters.

I mow the field
in what is left of the field—
goldenrod at the fence-line

where the rabbit hid, I burn
what is left. My trees
turn to soot. Soot

of goldenrod at the fence-line.
Hollyhocks in what is left
of the field—soot on pink,

soot on red, on white.
Hollyhock. Hollyhock.
The rasp of my voice—

a small sooty sound.
I plant flowers. We are
now, township by township

rough at the edges, trees
snapped, brush burning—
early in this summer

of the old trees blowing down.

II

M Y T H

The woman in the ordinary
cloth—came here with a vision:
point and counterpoint

in all things. Stitch by stitch
she wove our world—print
of pear tree, color of moss

delighted. Colors of silk.
Outside, the crack in the pathway
opened, rain spilled in—*tomorrow*

said the rivulets, *sorrow*
to the seas. Homeless, homeless—
heaved the low sky. Mist

entered the garden. Twilight
entered the mist. Lemon-cut
of the geranium lifted too.

She did not want the scent, she
wanted the blossom. But the blossom
faded in the fading light

and the clear voice of leaves
then said *it is all just wrestling*
and turning—before the windows

of the dead: And the geranium,
and the mist, and the pear tree—
all shifted slightly in a single wind.

Before the First Errand

(—which was her life on earth)
there were the practice moments:
the stars from no perspective,

the stockyards in winter. Thud
of mallet on skull—from no
perspective. In this way

she came to sense a manner of
being she wasn't there for:
the wide burst of pigeons

at dawn was not enough to keep her
from being carried in whatever
direction the changing wind suggested.

But eventually—she sensed her boy
had passed under the leviathan's
jawbone into the graveyard overlooking

the sea. She knew there was no way
to reach him, knew he would
lie on his mother's grave forever—

stunned beyond all reason, unconsoled,
that gray-as-the-answer would enter.

And the hills are messy with golden stalks.
The gray of the ocean is with him always.
The reddish fall vines, and the grave of the sky.

Shadow Day

She never even asked him
not to paint them, she
knows *no-point-in-asking*

when she meets it—she
only asked that he count
the bodies, particularly

the children, bodies
or heads—but history
is myth in the making,

history is water
he told her. She wanted
hard facts, he gave her

the world in motion.

THE COMPLEXITY OF MUSIC

At the bottom of music
a phrase is missing:
The white mist is coming

or *We shall be as if deserted*—.
Ocean all around us,
ocean and white mist—

(a cavern of darkness
where the phrase is missing
at the bottom of music)

where a phrase is missing.
From the floor of the ocean
a song goes out as vibration—

the water resists.
At this depth the song
has no chance. The woman

who waits for the song
will disappear into waiting.
At this depth the song

has no chance—save
she is at the bottom
of a phrase in the ocean

and the music around her—
is known as dark water.

WAS LIGHT

at the bottom
there, tomorrow,—

else where I
missed it? *And*

where I missed it?

Luna in the House of All My Longing

Scrub this world clean.
Begin with a dream.
Do you even dream.

Enter the house
of magnolia. Enter
the magnolia tree.

See? So she
puts her arms up,
wiggles her fingers,

moths and butterflies
butterflies and moths.
She performs a plea.

With Fruit Loop dust
all over her face—
who can resist her?

We enter the house of magnolia.
We enter the blossom.
We enter the tree.

Hint

And what about
the life of the body?
Is there *there* a single grief

you will believe in?
There are geraniums
on the doorstep, bug-eaten

at the blossom and at
the leaf: you can pinch off
the dead parts, you can

water, you can turn away—
but you cannot stop yourself.

The Habit of Resistance

That toxic drive—
a pure urge
of sorts: numbers

as numbers, function
in progress. Each fall
a new beginning.

The wings in the trees
are black. The buildings
crumble, the asphalt

cracks. Every spring
we count the dead:
The unlucky. Sometimes

we call them the lucky.
The years: a melody
of the lucky: a curtain

of lace, a wing
of sorts. Make no mistake—
each time we cry. What

do the weeds know, where
is the justification
for the weeks, the endlessness

of days, the incorruptible
urge: Function in progress?
Numbers as numbers?

The wings in the trees
are black, the fear
in the wings comes back—

endlessness of days
and then the end.
We itemize our

tenderness, we itemize
our dead. Make
no mistake—each time

we cry. We carry
our grief whole, we
carry our lives. Swayed

by the under-self,
it's how we love.

PRINCE OF FIRE PRINCE

Though the almanac hang
between us, though my brow
and my hands are maps—

I will encircle you
as I encircle you now
when my brow and my hands

are ash. We will be
as if chosen. Even the air
will have to pretend.

On the Shores of Rivers and Seas We Admire Our Thinking

We make rules and think by them—
and call it *good* thinking: Foundation.
Structure: We think the river

runs *by* not *through*: the current—
dispensable, the shore—coincidence,
the sky—a margin, a margin

with far limits, but a margin.
Our symposium on the question
assumes the viewer—some seas being

too salty to believe in. We *do*
ask many questions. Whoever
wants to answer, answers: this is not

based on seaweed and trees. It is
based on knowledge—which is based
on seaweed and trees. There is

also falseness: the true sky,
for example, doesn't always
figure in,—some seas being too salty.

THE HIGH HITHER, THE EMBRACE

The stairs to the marketplace where we were
all going to speak the same language—were littered
with the elaborate cruelties of history,

the injustice of water, the shed and chasm
side by side. The stairs to the experiment
in which I meant to convince you we spoke

the same language—were our unleashing:
a dream in prose in which I'm trying
to miss you. But history will have none of this,

as far back as I can hear it: The mudflats
usher in tadpoles and onion grass: the sweet,
sweet earth, aroused.—The Empire ushers in flesh:

The high hither: the you: the embrace.

It Was Not Anything After All?

Thus the wind and the dark
sage sea. Thus the wingèd wave
means *you can't have it*. And the dark

stars and the light stars too—
irreversible heavens, earthly butcher,
invisible shadow, bilge-pump,—you.

The butcher says later
is soon enough. He looks for a stone
to sharpen his blade. All manner

of knowing pushes up, out of
visibly nowhere,—and essential:
mindlessness and seagulls, trembling

and clean: we wore our Easter bonnets
and prayed. Mother booked a ticket
to the islands—extravagant picnic

by the dark sage sea. Mother says later
is soon enough, all manner of knowing
pushes up, out of visibly nowhere—and clean.

The World Holding Out

It was given us
to see and, seeing, know

wholeness in the dog
in chase, familiarity

in the rabbit's cry,—
signature of blood on snow.

That Which Came of Nothing Coming Always

I have been hearing
the wind in this stand
of white pines ever

since I heard it
for the first time.
I have been hearing

the small fast river—
bright din beneath which
the waters splinter

off smooth rocks. I
have been hearing
this icy symphony

ever since I heard it
for the first time.
We are two women, walking

toward an unclaimed
expanse of horizon,
the fray of history

all around us—
and we carry everything:
the fragmentation of water,

stalactite I buried
with Willa, here
on Tina's farm where

we're half hidden
in the white pines, half
loving the icy wind.

THE WOMAN WHOSE
SPECIALTY IS LIGHT —

weathers a marsh of darkness:
night like a smudge, the day-moon
disappearing with the day,

the night-moon never coming.
Fog in the cattails is born here.
Details from an origin for the woman

whose specialty is light—light
as a book left open, the page
random, the thought she

returns to—looking for choice.
And if she gives this bruise-light
back, if she neglects the working

night, neglects the cattails,
swamp or fog—she will lose them
for now and for always, back into

the house of maps. Light
in halos, light plowing off
the dawn, pawing at the edges

of this very day—dispersing.

Seventy Feet from the Magnolia Blossom

there is an ant.

He is carrying
a heavy load.—

We should help him.

Gypsum When You Arrive

For just as there is alabaster
in the marketplace there is
the remembrance of gypsum

in the sun,—when the body
watches. If you listen
you will turn toward a remote

and ancient calling: *alien:*
you survive: beyond the brownish air
around the globe, another

streaked sky waits—as if for
a *flickering-of-wings* which it cannot
contain. As if for the flinch

in your voice.—Which it can.

The Crypt of the House

that she was born in echoes
larger than the house itself
ever was. As a girl, summers

every morning for years,
she carried the small dog
down to the river and sang

and sang to her. This much
is still available: it is
no wonder that the light

was laced—there were trees
everywhere along the banks.
No wonder that she didn't

have a name for what
compelled her: in fall
the patterns of geese

told a story about patterns
of geese in spring. The girl
charmed the world, she made

what she saw into something
to see her. The woman
lies in wait on the banks—

endless study in fracture
and repair, crypt of nooks
crypt of crannies. The light

is green, but the map
of that county is torn along
the line where the river ran.

THE ORIGIN

of what happened is not in language—
of this much I am certain.
Six degrees south, six east—

and you have it: the bird
with the blue feathers, the brown bird—
same white breasts, same scaly

ankles. The waves between us—
house light and transform motion
into the harboring of sounds in language.—

Where there is newsprint
the fact of desire is turned from again—
and again. Just the sense

that what remains might well be held up—
later, as an ending.
Twice I have walked through this life—

once for nothing, once
for facts: fairy-shrimp in the vernal pool—
glassy-winged sharpshooter

on the failing vines. Count me—
among the animals, their small
committed calls.—

Count me among
the living. My greatest desire—
to exist in a physical world.

WAS LIGHT, —

was next week with a garden
in it, next winter with the glow
of the unborn. My back

up against the mountain, face
to the snowy field,—glassy
branches of the apple tree.

If there was a mistake somewhere
I didn't know it, I only knew
the deodar choked on sky,—despite

the rumor of unaltered roots.
The essential and noble
insects burrowed. Blades

of grass mixed with snow.
I only know there is limited
liability for each party—:

the integrated lives of ants
and geese, the upturned
feet of dead rodents: corrupt

parade—as in this labor
leads to blood in the heart.
Water running over the grave.

The light drives forth
inside the head. Inside
and outside. Two beams

which must now intersect.

THE KNOWING-SHORE

The calamity at Babel
aside, the science
of the greater

and of the lesser
lights aside, and all
the abundance and terror

of commerce between
men of the products
of nature and art

aside, there are still
to consider the cones
of the deodar, turning

as they do turn,—
purple in the fall
in the southeastern

United States, but not
on the Left Coast
where they stay green

longer, through
winter even, so that
we could, then, still,

couldn't we, take it
for a sacred
mission after all,

the garden, its terse
violet, violent
rose, Rose of Sharon—

or is it only that
in a form of knowing
since abandoned,

the wish went out
and the thought
received, habit

of world made
habit of mind—
but that now: violet,

rose, purple
cones, *desolate*
theme park,—desire

aside now, life
of my life, heart
of my heart,—abandoned?

To the Wren, No Difference
No Difference to the Jay

I came a long
way to believe
in the blue jay

and I did not cheat
anyone. I
came a long way—

through complexities
of bird-sound and calendar
to believe in nothing

before I believed
in the jay.

III

THE LADEN HENCEFORTH PENDING

My assignment was *one useful plan,*
to make one useful plan of the surrounding
thirteen hundred acres of chaparral

and oak, manzanita and bunchgrass
in the season of the oak's unfurling,
in the season of the blue-eyed grasses,

wind-washed and rain-swept and moving
toward the scorch of summer,—*make*
an afternoon of it, he said.

Three dogs came with me up the hill
named for its sugar-pines, to what
we call the *little pike*—that farthest

meadow of my childhood,—the red head
of the vulture bent with watching,
the red tail of the hawk spread wide.

Your memory casts a shadow when you
go into the future, and the shadow
wants to know what owns you—the red

and lichened trunk of the madrona
or the twin dry creeks converging as matter
and lack of matter meeting. You have to be

nothing, take whatever amnesty is offered—
the case for love is not the case
for tragedy revisited, or there is

for certain now—a laden henceforth pending.

Trans-Generational Haunting

They come to you in dreams,
the dearly departed. They
come to you again and again—
elsewhere and otherwise included.

The same.

Then facing the purple mountain
and her shadow, I am watching
to keep them from slipping away.

I look inward—
I look outward—
all the same.

I was loved.
I was loved
and I return—

everywhere the dead
calling my name.

THE FLESH IS FEAR

and the compass—unfettered
by true north. The sky
hangs open—to breathe

is to shift just a little
toward earth, necessary
earth,—recounting for all

it is worth the problematic
acting-out of air, the flaw
in the green of the forest.

Not careful, not loyal.
Keep going the wind.
An event worth noting.

The singer of virtues
travels the short line back
from diamonds to coal—.

Keep silence, she says,
keep luck—some great thing
is crossing our path, into dusk.

LIMINAL

Where the yellow thistle
comes into its own,
home to bunchgrass,

oak, madrone, where
the hunters set out
for the bridge across

eternity, *buckeye*
antler, bone,—your
deer-colored dog

is loping in the
deer-colored grass
in the morning. *Nowhere*

are you where we are not.

SAME AUDIT, SAME SACRIFICE

I spent half my life talking to you
and I never got an answer. That's a kind
of sailing you wouldn't call sailing

unless you had to. I wanted to know
about the earth and the sea—about
the unleashed moments. I marked the days,

I measured the snowfall, in summer
I washed my feet in buckets. In fall
while other people were sporting

bright sweaters and carrying home
bags of tomatoes, I watched
the shadow of the barges, watched

the dragging of the river,
the moment and the specter—then
I took the selfsame audit.

H E A R T

(S N O W   F A L L I N G)

Heart, no matter what door you return through—
inches falling,—in pitch of night confettied,
in dawn-light: no matter: I will put you out

over and again until what matters most—
the not knowing of what I do not know—
rises in the now moonlight as the final inch

begins to crust toward shine and I speak so:
Go out, heart, into it. Do not return. Because mine
is a body caught, because submit is not your answer—

and because you, like the enchanted moon, are good.

HIGH CLIFF COMING

Fate's a stable lesson
after all: the trees
can't grow into the

prevailing wind—the
bird-like hands
can't fly.

Where the waves fold back
and the high cliff guides—
this elegy

keeps the heart
beating and the blood
from going cold

while the nerves
web the body—
the body-dream.

SOMETIMES THE MIND

is taken by surprise
as it speaks: *are you
sure this is the right street?*

for example—or just
cow-path—no more: a blurb,
a bleep, really, out of

the imagination, and then
once again everything is
perfectly still, save, perhaps,

a cow or two on the horizon,—
and the sound of cowbirds
in sudden excellence, where

formerly there were none.

With No Praise
from the Far Dark Reaches

I believe in the horse and the marshes—I believe
in the crow,—talisman of apple tree and pear.
I believe in the wall. This wall and the other.

Did I say the willow? I believe the willow
knows what the dead know, passing over.

Unmeasurable dust from here to the nearest star—

keep circling, for if I believe in our mutual
intervals of response and longing, all the more
do I believe in how the animals take themselves

somewhat sadly off into the shrubbery and damp grasses
toward the roughly longed-for passage. The Tradition.

The grasses. I believe in the dust and the grasses.

SPECULATION

I do not think that love will reach the dead—
and, the seven weeks of sorrow pending,
I do not think they should have much regret:
the marginalia and mania survive them
and that was all they might have taken.

My own destiny is hard enough to salvage
from the safety pins, the thin discs of soap—
the plenty and the lack converging, the left hand
of the dead laid over the right hand
of the living, the left hand of the living
laid over the right hand of the dead.

I do not think the shadow of the cloud
is sign, until the hawk lays *his* shadow down.
I have no proof the dead survive the call.

In Grief
the Pilot Knows You

In grief, the pilot knows you—
no need to say *take me to my so-called soul*—
she *is* your so-called soul: she knows
you will be waiting when she lands—she wants
you to be with her if you drown.

In the spring, we lost our innocence

and took center stage. Fall
was the time of harvest, just as in summer
there was bounty in the wind-sound
and the farmer-self learning her lessons

from the vines and then the rows of vines—
bounty in the one voice joined
to the multitude of its own becoming.

In winter, the grit on the wind is the single
candor we live by—and while the far shore
and the cliffs beyond it are fogged in—

it does not occur to us to weep:
a shore is not a shore without her.

LABYRINTH

Tomorrow,—by reason of rapture.
Rapture—by reason of pain.
There is tomorrow in it

and we look away.
There is tomorrow in the one
God-given stone, and we look away.

When we look away we look into
the past. We get down on our knees
in sorrow. We are much too stunned

to pray. The truth about today
was a bright stone shining—.
By reason of nightmare, by reason

of pain, by reason of wit revisited.
By reason of madness, whosoever
begins shall be asked to finish.

The Woman in the Ordinary Cloth

came here with a mission.
Work by work there starts a world
that the vines and poppies finish.

At night the coyote songs
stir a vision: the vineyard
and the grave are one. By day

the dead inhabit the canyons,
the living weed the vine-rows
and she wanders between them—

calls the months *bunchgrass, thistle
coyote-brush.* Afternoons on the hillside
two large madrones create the circle

of shade in which she is now sleeping.

THE SPECTER AND HIS WORLD ARE ONE

Some say a jar can tell you
where you are, some say
a satellite. Others—

the postman, the stars,
the sea. It is possible
for the world to mislead you.

You cannot look too much
over your shoulder.
The symbol for moss

is a symbol for destiny:
The shut blaze darkens.
The world misleads you.

You cannot look too much
over your shoulder, I
cannot but say now

follow me,—onto the road
my own heart made,—
the red disc—

the real clay—
pile of yellow thistle
where I'm weeding.

This is the red earth *you* loved
—my way into.

(*for my father, in memoriam*)

Where in the Story the Horse Mazy Dies

&

Anymore the rain that matters, anymore the thistle.
And never matter the *word* as a way of being for:
In the era of *postmodern* and *maybe*

the mammals still strike up friendships.
I let the vines cover these windows on purpose.
Neither laziness nor doubt—but memory.

I was the wind, and the needle she went for.
I was the bridge and halt to elsewhere—
and the book that told the lie survives.

Eagle topping the deodar, barn owls in the palms,
moss on the roof where the old shed sags.
The magpie will be here for the tree-green act.

Thistle, weevil, rain—whoever prays, prays.
Ever the green door opens, you must go there.

&

At Big Creek, celestial creaking—canopy-light,
world greening and the river-white sound.
I knew no lullabies but sang her a story

where in the story the horse Mazy dies—
where she would go, what hope unfolding,
what mind concluding down around her.

Forage the wet forage. Forage the dry.
She was a bit of birdsong her stubborn self—
in rule of point and passage, in point of being.

And the skinny cow-faced dog is rat now
and the grassy puddles tremble in the rain.

&
Also I penned a delicate engine, green wash over.
Saw several mysteries unfolding—*Gracie Gracie Gracie:*
barn owls in the palm tree (heads on shoulders) sleeping.

Book says *Not ever three grown owls in a single tree*!!
Three Gracies say *maybe well a* PALM *tree*.
Maybe not MAYBE the Gracies say,—

or why would anyone draw an engine ever now?
Where will I go with my engine, my unfolding.
In rule of great and thick, in rule of passage—

wand, prayer, deck of cards, revolver—
why would anyone ever draw an engine now?

&
If I wanted to know what the birds want
I should have paid attention to the book,
it being late in the history of study.

Still—what kind of bird would just stand there
under the sun for mad dogs, pecking at rocks
where once the birdbath sat,—bird stupid.

&

That bloody sickle is our moon, the hills are black.
The chickens have broken their own warm eggs,
the chickens have feasted on yolk.

Sleep leaves the barn owls and their phantom chicks.
Ghost-bodies speaking: this is the wind they came for.
The sound of fronds on the sky in the wind—

sound they stayed for. Body in mind-darkness.
Ministry of fog forgotten. Ministry of hunger.
Bloody sickle, hills black. The owl is stirring.

The night is a hunting night. The night is a dark door.
Ever the green door opens—*fly*.

&
Solitude of all remembrance, magnitude of knowing—
holding your muzzle I let you go down, dust—
you were a fading light then, a disappearing blaze.

Out in the open by the backhoe, Mazy
move clockwise, move counter. Moss persisting—
trough of brown water where you and the Dane drank—

murky water where the small dog swims.
Corral-dust, trough of red film settling unforgiven.
Remembering your look from a long way in.

Remembering the slow shut, then gaze returned.
Mazy leave your smell now, leave your ribbon.
Leave a plain-stay Mazy, once: your look returning.

Shut the sky darkens, shut darkens the aftermath.
With the buzzards you are not now *nowhere* circling.

&

We will calm and craze, begin another *never*.
Not the language of renewal, nor the *nothing-to-retrieve*.
For the *meant* of history lies in the seen.

Mathematics of rain on snow, for example.
Or the strategy of birds across the globe.
Or *we are not a spectator sport* say the chickens.

I brought home mustard-flower and little legumes,
small arguments home from their home in the vineyard—
for the sub-arguments of the moving mind are endless.

I let the vines cover these windows on purpose.
The bird outside is another story.

&
Chimera of shapes in neutral where the old molds break.
Chimera of things revisited will go to any length—
forgetting with remembrance at its cusp. I did it.

I did it not so long ago for unheard voices.
I did it not so long ago for scientific voices.
She was no small entrustment—I had my reasons.

The bridge and halt to later—unforgiving.
Unforgiving—the tillage in its earnest rows of clot.
The *maybe* with its next of kin the *therefore*—

land of concur and stone I am not that *I-did-it*.
Also, I am here of my own choosing.

Notes

⤲

"Gift Horizon": *Turn the head of the bird*: Just before his death, Renoir is said to have uttered these words. The poem is not specifically about Renoir.

"The High Hither, The Embrace": The title of this poem is taken from a phrase in a poem by Paul Celan.

"That Which Came of Nothing/Coming Always" is for Tina Bourjaily.

"The Crypt of the House" is for Carter Smith.

"The Woman Whose Specialty Is Light—" is for my mother.

"Liminal" and "The Flesh is Fear" are for Graham de Freitas.

RECENT TITLES FROM
ALICE JAMES BOOKS

King Baby, Lia Purpura
The Temple Gate Called Beautiful, David Kirby
Door to a Noisy Room, Peter Waldor
Beloved Idea, Ann Killough
The World in Place of Itself, Bill Rasmovicz
Equivocal, Julie Carr
A Thief of Strings, Donald Revell
Take What You Want, Henrietta Goodman
The Glass Age, Cole Swensen
The Case Against Happiness, Jean-Paul Pecqueur
Ruin, Cynthia Cruz
Forth A Raven, Christina Davis
The Pitch, Tom Thompson
Landscapes I & II, Lesle Lewis
Here, Bullet, Brian Turner
The Far Mosque, Kazim Ali
Gloryland, Anne Marie Macari
Polar, Dobby Gibson
Pennyweight Windows: New & Selected Poems, Donald Revell
Matadora, Sarah Gambito
In the Ghost-House Acquainted, Kevin Goodan
The Devotion Field, Claudia Keelan
Into Perfect Spheres Such Holes Are Pierced, Catherine Barnett
Goest, Cole Swensen
Night of a Thousand Blossoms, Frank X. Gaspar
Mister Goodbye Easter Island, Jon Woodward
The Devil's Garden, Adrian Matejka
The Wind, Master Cherry, the Wind, Larissa Szporluk
North True South Bright, Dan Beachy-Quick
My Mojave, Donald Revell
Granted, Mary Szybist
The Captain Lands in Paradise, Sarah Manguso

Alice James Books has been publishing exclusively poetry since 1973. One of the few presses in the country that is run collectively, the cooperative selects manuscripts for publication through both regional and national annual competitions. New regional authors become active members of the cooperative, participating in the editorial decisions of the press. The press, which historically has placed an emphasis on publishing women poets, was named for Alice James, sister of William and Henry, whose fine journal and gift for writing went unrecognized within her lifetime.

TYPESET AND DESIGNED BY
DEDE CUMMINGS

Printed by Thomson-Shore
on 50% postconsumer recycled paper
processed chlorine-free